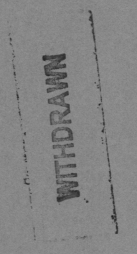

Out and About at the Orchestra

Field Trips

Written by Barbara J. Turner • Illustrated by Anne McMullen

Content Advisor: Jennifer Marble
Director of Marketing and Communications, New Hampshire Symphony Orchestra, Manchester, New Hampshire

Reading Advisor: Lauren A. Liang, M.A.
Literacy Education, University of Minnesota, Minneapolis, Minnesota

PICTURE WINDOW BOOKS
Minneapolis, Minnesota

For my kids—Rich, Christina, and Gina, who make the music in my life—B.J.T

Thanks to New Hampshire Symphony Orchestra and Jennifer Marble, Director of Marketing and Communications.

Designer: Melissa Voda
Page production: Picture Window Books
The illustrations in this book were rendered using watercolor and ink.

Picture Window Books
5115 Excelsior Boulevard
Suite 232
Minneapolis, MN 55416
1-877-845-8392
www.picturewindowbooks.com

Printed in the United States of America.
1 2 3 4 5 6 08 07 06 05 04 03

Library of Congress Cataloging-in-Publication Data
Turner, Barbara J.
  Out and about at the orchestra / written by Barbara J. Turner ; illustrated by Anne McMullen.
    p. cm. Includes index.
  Summary: Examines the instruments that make up an orchestra, their arrangement on the stage, the role of the conductor, and the need of the musicians to practice.
  ISBN 1-4048-0040-9 (lib. bdg. : alk. paper)
  1. Orchestra—Juvenile literature. [1. Orchestra. 2. Musical instruments.] I. McMullen, Anne, ill. II. Title.
  ML1200 .T87 2003
  784.2—dc21

2002006289

We're going on a field trip to the orchestra. We can't wait!

Things to find out:
Why does the orchestra always sit in a half circle?
What's a woodwind instrument?
Who chooses what music to play?
Do musicians practice every day?

Welcome to the orchestra. I'm Anna, your tour guide.

You're in for a grand tour and a great performance.

4   Please pick up your tickets and follow me.

A ticket usually lists a row and a seat number, such as Row B, Seat 25. To find their seats, concertgoers match the letter and number on their tickets to the row and seat number inside the concert hall.

This is the concert hall. Music travels from the musicians through the air in invisible sound waves. The waves bounce off the walls and ceiling. The walls and ceiling are built to help the music sound its best.

The musicians sit in a half-circle on stage. This shape makes the sounds of different instruments blend together. It also helps the musicians hear one another better.

7

Stringed instruments make up more than half of the orchestra.
Watch these musicians move their bows across the strings.
Stringed instruments can make sounds as soft as a trickling stream
or as loud as a thunderstorm. Sometimes the string players pluck
8   the strings with their fingers to make short, popping sounds.

Each stringed instrument is played with a bow. The bows are strung tightly with hairs from horse tails. When a musician pulls the bow over an instrument's strings, the strings shake, or vibrate. The music you hear is the sound of the vibrating strings. The smaller stringed instruments have a higher sound. The larger ones sound lower and deeper.

9

A woodwind is a long, tube-like instrument that a musician plays by blowing through it. Woodwinds can sound light and airy, or dark and scary. Listen for the high sounds of the shorter instruments and the low sounds of the longer ones.

A reed is a thin piece of cane. Cane is a stiff plant, like bamboo.
Reeds fit in the mouthpieces of clarinets, oboes, and bassoons.
When a musician blows through a reed, it vibrates and makes sound.

11

The brass instruments boom and blare. Horns howl and trumpets blast, while tubas bellow and trombones moan. Sometimes brass players want to make quieter sounds. Then, they place a mute inside the bell, or wide end, of their instrument.

Many brass instruments and woodwinds have keys, or buttons. Pressing a key changes the distance the air travels through the instrument. The farther the air has to go, the lower the sound will be.

Percussion instruments are played by striking or shaking them.
If you can bang it like a drum, ring it like a bell, or jingle it like
a tamborine, the instrument belongs in this section.

Percussion instruments come from all over the world, in all shapes and sizes: Chinese gongs, Turkish cymbals, Cuban bongos, Spanish maracas and castanets, African drums, and steel drums from the West Indies.

The conductor is the leader of the orchestra. During practices and performances, the conductor counts out the beat and keeps the musicians playing together. Conductors also choose the music and tell the musicians when to play faster or slower, louder or softer. Under the direction of a good conductor, the orchestra works together as a team.

A conductor's score, or sheet music, can be 30 or more pages long. It shows the parts for each musician. For a performance, a conductor either memorizes all the parts or follows the parts by reading the score.

Now find your seats and pick up your programs. The concert is about to begin. Listen for how the strings, woodwinds, brass, and percussion instruments work together with the conductor to make amazing music.

A program is filled with information about the music played at a concert. It names the people who wrote the music and the musicians who will be playing.

19

A good performance can paint pictures in your mind and fill you with wonderful new feelings. We hope you enjoyed this special concert.

Orchestra musicians lead busy lives. Many travel from city to city, playing in different orchestras. Some musicians have second jobs as music teachers. They find time to practice, no matter how busy they are. They practice every day. Musicians work hard, because they love making music.

21

MAKE YOUR OWN PERCUSSION INSTRUMENT:

A Rain Stick

The rain stick is a percussion instrument that comes from South America. The first rain sticks were made from a piece of cactus that was turned inside out, dried, and filled with pebbles. The pebbles sounded like rain as they tapped against the cactus needles inside. People believed the rain gods would hear the sound of the rain stick and answer their prayers for rain. Now, rain sticks are used mostly in orchestras and bands to add a South American sound.

What you need

an empty paper towel tube

wax paper

1 or 2 plastic berry containers, the kind with holes in them

1 cup uncooked rice

2 rubber bands

masking tape

scissors

crayons or markers

What you do

1. Cut two circles of wax paper larger than the openings of the paper towel tube.
2. Cover one end of the tube with a circle of wax paper. Place a rubber band around the wax paper to hold it in place. Wrap masking tape over the rubber band and the loose edges of the wax paper.
3. Cut the berry containers into pieces just small enough to fit inside the tube. Fill the tube with as many pieces as you can. Use a pencil or ruler to shove the pieces deep inside the tube.
4. Pour in the rice. You may have to shake the rain stick to get all the rice inside.
5. Cover the open end of the tube with the second circle of wax paper. Secure it with a rubber band and masking tape just as you did in Step 2.
6. Color or decorate your rain stick.
7. Turn your rain stick upside down and listen to it rain.

FUN FACTS

- Musicians do not wear jewelry to a performance. Bracelets and necklaces might make jingling noises or get caught on their instruments. The musicians wear black so people will pay attention to the music and not the musicians' clothes.

- Large orchestras, such as the Boston Symphony and the New York Philharmonic, might have up to 100 musicians playing at once.

- Musicians who practice six hours a day for 20 years will have spent 5 years of their lives practicing. In a 100-piece orchestra, that adds up to 500 years of practice.

- Conductors use their hands or a small stick called a baton to keep the beat of the music. Long ago, conductors used a huge stick that they banged on the floor.

- Musicians who play large instruments, such as the double bass or tuba, buy airplane seats for their instruments when they travel. If a musician checked an instrument with the luggage, it could get broken.

- Concert halls have not always been just for concerts. In its early days, Boston's Symphony Hall was also used for wrestling matches and chicken shows.

- Not all musicians have to hear music in order to play it. Some percussion players are deaf. They perform without wearing shoes so they can feel the music's vibrations through the stage.

WORDS TO KNOW

brass instruments—musical instruments made of brass or other metals, which are played by blowing into the mouthpiece

keys—buttons on instruments that close holes or guide airflow

mute—a piece added to an instrument to soften the sound; the act of softening sound

percussion instruments—musical instruments such as drums, cymbals, and tambourines, which are played by hitting, banging, ringing, rattling, or scratching

pluck—to pull back a string on a stringed instrument and snap it, producing a short, popping sound

program—a document that tells who will be playing at a concert and what they will play

score—the written notes for a musical work, showing the parts for each instrument and giving instructions on how the notes should be played

stringed instruments—musical instruments with strings, which are played by drawing a bow across the strings or plucking the strings with the fingers

woodwinds—instruments usually made of wood, which are played by blowing into the mouthpiece. Except for the flute and piccolo, woodwinds are made of wood and have a reed in the mouthpiece that vibrates when the instrument is played.

TO LEARN MORE

At the Library

Koscielniak, Bruce. *The Story of the Incredible Orchestra.* Boston: Houghton Mifflin Co., 2000.

Lithgow, John. *The Remarkable Farkle McBride.* New York: Simon & Schuster, 2000.

Moss, Lloyd. *Zin! Zin! Zin! A Violin.* New York: Simon & Schuster, 1995.

Rau, Dana Meachen. *Making Music.* Minneapolis: Compass Point Books, 2002.

On the Web

The Dallas Symphony Orchestra

http://www.dsokids.com

For musical fun and learning from the Dallas Symphony Orchestra

The Baltimore Symphony Orchestra

http://www.bsokids.com

For musical games, a backstage tour, Fun Facts, and more from the Baltimore Symphony Orchestra

Want to learn more about the orchestra? Visit FACT HOUND at *http://www.facthound.com.*

INDEX

baton, 23
bow, 8–9
brass instruments, 12–13, 18
clothing of musicians, 23
concert hall, 6–7, 23
conductor, 16–17, 23
mute, 12
percussion instruments, 14–15, 18, 22
practice, 21, 23
program, 18–19
reed, 11
sound waves, 6
stage, 7
stringed instruments, 8–9, 18
tickets, 4–5
woodwinds, 10–11, 18